LEMURS

by Jaclyn Jaycox

PEBBLE
a capstone imprint

Pebble Explore is published by Pebble, an imprint of Capstone.
1710 Roe Crest Drive
North Mankato, Minnesota 56003
www.capstonepub.com

Library of Congress Cataloging-in-Publication data is available on the Library of Congress website.
ISBN 978-1-9771-2316-9 (library binding)
ISBN 978-1-9771-2650-4 (paperback)
ISBN 978-1-9771-2324-4 (eBook PDF)

Summary: Text describes lemurs, including where they live, their bodies, what they do, and dangers to lemurs.

Image Credits
Alamy: imageBROKER, 19; Capstone Press, 6; iStockphoto: Hajakely, 25; Newscom: Gerald Cubitt/NHPA/Photoshot, 13; Shutterstock: Angyalosi Beata, 18, Arto Hakola, 5, Carl Jones Photography, 20, Damian Ryszawy, 12, David C Azor, 21, Hajakely, 9, Jordi Prat Puig, 28, KRISS75, 27, MicheleB, 7, MyImages - Micha, 14, Ondrej Chvatal, 22, Ondrej Prosicky, 15, Ondrej_Novotny_92, Cover, 8, ONGUSHI, 17, Philippe Clement, 1, Sergey Didenko, 26, yakub88, 11

Editorial Credits
Editor: Mandy Robbins; Designer: Dina Her; Media Researcher: Morgan Walters; Production Specialist: Tori Abraham

All internet sites appearing in back matter were available and accurate when this book was sent to press.

Printed in the United States of America.
PA117

Table of Contents

Words in **bold** are in the glossary.

Amazing Lemurs

What is that furry animal jumping through the trees? It's a lemur! They spend most of their time above the ground. They move easily through the trees. They can jump six times their body length!

There are more than 100 kinds of lemurs. They are **mammals**. Mammals breathe air. They have hair or fur. Females feed milk to their young.

Where in the World

Lemurs are found off the coast of Africa. They live in Madagascar and the Comoros Islands. This is the only part of the world lemurs are found.

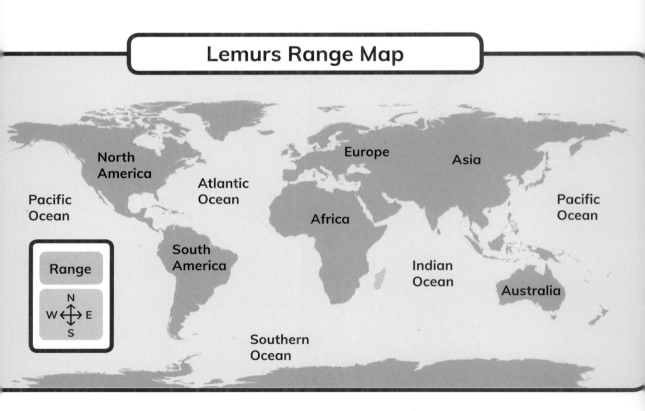

Lemurs Range Map

North America

Europe

Asia

Pacific Ocean

Atlantic Ocean

Pacific Ocean

Africa

South America

Indian Ocean

Australia

Range

N
W ⟷ E
S

Southern Ocean

Lemurs have lived there for more than 50 million years. Some scientists believe they once lived in Africa. They may have floated to Madagascar on logs.

Lemurs live in many different kinds of **habitats**. Some live in dry forests. Others live in hot, wet **rain forests**. They can also be found in wetlands such as swamps. Some live in mountains.

Most lemurs live high up in trees. They eat and sleep there. Other lemurs spend almost half their time on the ground.

Lemur Bodies

Lemurs have long, furry tails. Most lemurs have tails that are longer than their bodies. They use them for balance. They also use them to steer when jumping between trees.

Ring-tailed lemurs have black and white striped tails. They use them to **communicate**. They wave them in the air. This helps other lemurs find them.

Lemurs can have white, brown, or black fur. They can have gray or reddish fur too.

indri lemur

Madame Berthe's mouse lemur

Lemurs are many different sizes. Madame Berthe's mouse lemur is the smallest. It is about the size of a mouse. It weighs about 1 ounce (28 grams). The largest is the indri lemur. It can weigh up to 21 pounds (9.5 kilograms). That's as heavy as a car tire!

Lemurs use their hands and feet to jump from tree to tree. Lemurs have strong legs. Their hands are like human hands. They have four fingers and a thumb. They have special pads on their hands and feet. The pads help them grip tree branches.

Lemurs have big eyes and long, pointed noses. They see better at night than during the day. They don't see colors. But they do have a super sense of smell. They can recognize other lemurs by their scents.

On the Menu

An aye-aye lemur listens closely. It hears bugs moving under the tree bark. It chews a hole with its sharp teeth. The lemur grabs the bugs with its long finger. Dinner time!

Some kinds of lemurs eat bugs. Sometimes they even eat birds. Other lemurs do not eat meat. They eat fruits and leaves. They eat flowers and tree bark too.

Madagascar has wet and dry seasons. From May to October, little rain falls. Food is hard to find then.

Lemurs eat a lot in the wet season. They fill up while they can. Some eat nearly half their body weight!

fat-tailed dwarf lemur

Fat-tailed dwarf lemurs **hibernate**. They store fat in their tails. They go to sleep when the dry season comes. They live off their stored fat.

Life of a Lemur

Lemurs live in groups called troops. Troops travel together. They **groom** each other. They huddle together to keep warm.

Up to 25 lemurs live in a troop. Females stay in the same troop their whole lives. Males change troops every few years.

Lemurs make sounds to communicate. They scream to warn their troop of danger. They meow like cats. It helps them find each other.

Some lemurs build nests. Females give birth in them. Mothers usually give birth to one baby. Small lemurs can have up to six babies. Baby lemurs are called infants.

Babies can open their eyes right away. They hold on to their mothers' stomachs for the first month. Then they ride on their backs. At about four months, they can climb through the trees on their own.

Young lemurs drink milk from their mothers for up to six months. Other females help raise the young. Babies play together. By eight months old, they can take care of themselves. But they stay close to their mothers.

Males stay with their mother for about two years. Then they leave to join another group. Lemurs live up to 27 years.

Dangers to Lemurs

Lemurs don't have many **predators** that hunt them. The biggest one is a catlike animal called a fossa. Snakes and hawks hunt them too.

fossa

Humans are the greatest threat to lemurs. People cut down trees. At least 80 percent of Madagascar's forests have been destroyed. Lemurs are losing their homes and food.

Humans also hunt lemurs. Some people eat them. Others sell them as pets.

The number of lemurs is going down. They are the most **endangered** mammal in the world. But people are working to help. They are protecting the forests where they live. Laws are being passed to keep them from being hunted.

Fast Facts

Name: lemur

Habitat: dry forests, rain forests, mountains, and wetlands

Where in the World: Madagascar and the Comoros Islands

Food: fruit, leaves, tree bark, insects, birds, and flowers

Predators: fossas, snakes, hawks, and humans

Life span: up to 27 years

Glossary

communicate (kuh-MYOO-nuh-kate)—to share information, thoughts, or feelings

endangered (in-DAYN-juhrd)—at risk of dying out

groom (GROOM)—to clean and make an animal look neat

habitat (HAB-uh-tat)—the natural place and conditions in which a plant or animal lives

hibernate (HYE-bur-nate)—to spend an entire season in a deep sleep

mammal (MAM-uhl)—a warm–blooded animal that breathes air; mammals have hair or fur; female mammals feed milk to their young

predator (PRED-uh-tur)—an animal that hunts other animals for food

rain forest (RAYN FOR-ist)—a thick forest where rain falls nearly every day

Read More

Behrens, Ken. *Wildlife of Madagascar*. Princeton, NJ: Princeton University Press, 2016.

Cooper, Sharon Katz. *L Is for Lemur: ABCs of Endangered Primates*. North Mankato, MN: Capstone Press, 2017.

Gregory, Josh. *Lemurs*. New York: Scholastic Inc., 2017.

Internet Sites

Lemur Moms
climatekids.nasa.gov/lemurs/

Madagascar Lemurs for Kids
www.wildmadagascar.org/kids/08-wildlife-lemurs.html

Ring-tailed Lemur
kids.sandiegozoo.org/animals/ring-tailed-lemur

Index